Marcus Aurelius Meditations for Beginners

120-Day Stoic Journal

Charles Abbott

Disclaimer

This book and its contents are provided for educational purposes only and are not intended to replace or substitute any professional, medical, legal, or any other advice. The content contained herein presents the philosophy of Stoicism and is intended for educational purposes only.

While there are discussions related to coping with mental and physical health issues, and other life challenges, these are based on philosophical contemplation and personal insights from the perspective of Stoicism and should not be interpreted as medical, health, or psychological advice. If readers are facing medical conditions, mental health struggles, or personal crises, they are strongly encouraged to seek advice from qualified healthcare professionals or licensed therapists. The author and publisher specifically disclaim any responsibility for any liability, loss, or risk, personal or otherwise, that is incurred as a consequence, directly or indirectly, of the use and application of any of the contents of this book.

The author and publisher are not healthcare or mental health professionals, and the content presented should not be considered as medical or professional advice. The author and publisher are not liable for any errors, omissions, or inaccuracies in the content, or for any actions taken in reliance thereon. Furthermore, while the author has made every effort to ensure the accuracy and completeness of the information contained in this book, we apologize for any errors, omissions, or inconsistencies. Under no circumstances shall the author or publisher be liable for any special, direct, indirect, consequential, or incidental damages or any damages whatsoever, whether in an action of contract, negligence, or other torts, arising out of or in connection with the use of the content in this book. By continuing to read this book, you acknowledge and agree that you have fully understood this disclaimer and agree to use the information contained herein at your own risk and discretion.

Your Stoic Journey Supports Children in Need

In the pages that follow, not only will you embark on a journey of wonderful inner transformation and personal growth, but you will also be extending a hand of hope to children.

Our Commitment to Giving

This book is more than a literary endeavor; it is a heartfelt commitment to helping underprivileged children.

100% of the profits from Charlie's books are donated directly to charitable efforts dedicated to **helping children in need.**

Charles Abbott's books are published by Mei Service, a boutique publishing house with a vision to help children to learn one word, and one book at a time.

Join Us

To learn more about our initiatives and how your contribution is lighting up young lives, we welcome you to visit us at: www.meiservicebooks.com

Embark on a journey of wisdom, knowing that your path through these pages helps pave the way for a brighter tomorrow for the young ones we serve. Together, let's turn the act of reading into a legacy of hope.

Sign up for updates: https://subscribepage.io/stoicupdates

Table of Contents

Introduction

Welcome to your transformative journey through the wisdom of Stoicism, a path meticulously charted over the next 120 days.

This carefully planned journal, based on the profound meditations of Marcus Aurelius, is designed to serve as your guide and companion as you delve deep into the Stoic philosophy, applying its timeless principles to the complexities of modern life.

At the heart of this journey lies a commitment to personal growth and self-discovery. Each week, we embark on a thematic exploration, from understanding what lies within our control to embracing the virtues of Stoicism. These themes are not just philosophical concepts but are woven into the fabric of daily living, offering practical insights and tools to enhance every part of your life.

As you progress through each day, you will engage with a variety of topics, carefully chosen to deepen your understanding and practice of Stoic virtues.

This journey is structured to gradually build your knowledge and application of Stoicism, ensuring a comprehensive grasp of its teachings.

Each day brings a new focus, from cultivating inner peace to developing resilience, managing stress, and finding contentment in the simplest of things.

This journal is more than a mere collection of daily entries; it's a scaffolded approach to learning, reflecting, and growing. The questions posed each day are designed to probe your thoughts and beliefs, challenging you to reevaluate your perspectives and behaviors in the light of Stoic wisdom.

As you write, reflect, and ponder, you will find yourself developing a more profound sense of clarity, purpose, and serenity.

But the true beauty of this journey lies in its transformative power.

Stoicism teaches us not only to endure life's challenges but to thrive amidst them.

By embracing the Stoic principles, you will learn to find joy in adversity, strength in challenges, and wisdom in everyday experiences.

This journal will help you cultivate a mindset where happiness is not dependent on external circumstances but is a state of inner contentment and peace.

As you embark on this 120-day journey, remember that each entry is a step towards a more fulfilled, resilient, and enlightened self.

You are not just learning about Stoicism; you are embodying it, allowing its virtues to permeate your life, influencing your actions, decisions, and relationships.

This journal promises not just an intellectual understanding of Stoic philosophy but a profound personal transformation.

It's an invitation to a life of greater awareness, balance, and harmony.

So, open the first page, and let's begin this remarkable journey together, towards a life rich in wisdom, virtue, and happiness!

Your 120-Day Journey

Week 1: Understanding What is Within Your Control

- Day 1: The Dichotomy of Control
- Day 2: Accepting External Events
- Day 3: Inner Freedom
- Day 4: The Power of Perception
- Day 5: Taking Action Within Our Power
- Day 6: Responding to Others
- Day 7: Weekly Reflection on Control

Week 2: Cultivating Inner Peace

- Day 8: Peace Amidst Chaos
- Day 9: Serenity in the Self
- Day 10: Managing Anger
- Day 11: Overcoming Disturbances
- Day 12: The Role of Ego
- Day 13: Finding Calm
- Day 14: Weekly Reflection on Peace

Week 3: Embracing Change and Impermanence

- Day 15: The Nature of Change
- Day 16: Impermanence of Possessions
- Day 17: Life's Transitions
- Day 18: Embracing Mortality
- Day 19: Growth and Decay
- Day 20: Letting Go
- Day 21: Weekly Reflection on Change

Week 4: Pursuit of Wisdom

- Day 22: Defining Wisdom
- Day 23: The Wise Mindset
- Day 24: Learning from Others
- Day 25: Knowledge vs. Wisdom
- Day 26: The Philosopher King
- Day 27: The Folly of Ignorance
- Day 28: Weekly Reflection on Wisdom

Week 5: Developing Personal Virtue

- Day 29: Virtue as a Good
- Day 30: Honesty and Integrity
- Day 31: Courage in Daily Life
- Day 32: Justice and Fairness
- Day 33: Self-Discipline and Temperance

- Day 52: Pleasure vs. Contentment
- Day 53: The Internal Source of Happiness
- Day 54: Removing Desires
- Day 55: The Stoic and Society
- Day 56: Weekly Reflection on Happiness

Week 9: Relationships and Compassion

- Day 57: The Social Animal
- Day 58: Kindness and Compassion
- Day 59: Dealing with Difficult People
- Day 60: Forgiveness
- Day 61: The Community and the Individual
- Day 62: Love and Stoicism
- Day 63: Weekly Reflection on Relationships

Week 10: On Work and Duty

- Day 64: The Value of Labor
- Day 65: Duty and Discipline
- Day 66: Work as a Form of Virtue
- Day 67: Professional Challenges
- Day 68: Leadership and Stoicism
- Day 69: Ambition and Contentment
- Day 70: Weekly Reflection on Work

Week 11: Managing Emotions

- Day 71: Understanding Our Emotions
- Day 72: The Stoic and Anger
- Day 73: Stoicism and Fear
- Day 74: Dealing with Sadness
- Day 75: Envy and Jealousy
- Day 76: Euphoria and Equanimity
- Day 77: Weekly Reflection on Emotions

Week 12: The Reflective Practice

- Day 78: The Examination of Conscience
- Day 79: The Daily Review
- Day 80: Journaling as a Tool
- Day 81: The Role of Writing in Stoicism
- Day 82: Meditation and Reflection
- Day 83: Clarifying Thoughts Through Writing
- Day 84: Weekly Reflection on Practice

Week 13: Aligning with Nature

- Day 85: The Natural Order
- Day 86: Living According to Nature
- Day 87: The Rhythm of Life
- Day 88: Nature's Lessons
- Day 89: The Universe Within

- Day 90: Ecology and Stoicism
- Day 91: Weekly Reflection on Nature

Week 14: Preparation for Adversity

- Day 92: Premeditation of Evils
- Day 93: The Stoic's Armor
- Day 94: Facing Fears
- Day 95: Crisis and Character
- Day 96: The Unknown and the Uncontrollable
- Day 97: Anticipating Challenges
- Day 98: Weekly Reflection on Adversity

Week 15: The Practice of Asceticism

- Day 99: The Value of Ascetic Exercises
- Day 100: Minimalism and Purpose
- Day 101: Self-Denial and Strength
- Day 102: Luxury and Excess
- Day 103: Discipline of Desire
- Day 104: Enjoyment in Moderation
- Day 105: Weekly Reflection on Asceticism

Week 16: The Virtue of Contentment

- Day 106: Being Content with Little
- Day 107: Wealth and Happiness

- Day 108: Autarky - Self-Sufficiency
- Day 109: The True Value of Things
- Day 110: Independence from Materialism
- Day 111: Contentment in Action
- Day 112: Weekly Reflection on Contentment

Week 17: Justice and Society

- Day 113: The Just Life
- Day 114: Laws and Morals
- Day 115: The Social Contract
- Day 116: Actions and their Ripple Effects
- Day 117: Fairness in Practice
- Day 118: Stoicism in Leadership
- Day 119: Weekly Reflection on Justice and Society

Day 120: Looking Forward and Backward

- Reflection: A Comprehensive Review
- Moving Forward: Applying Stoic Principles to the Future

This journal serves as a daily guide with thoughtful content and probing questions that lead you on a progressive journey through Stoic philosophy as applied to modern life. By the end of 120 days, you'll be amazed at how far you've come and how much better your life is! Let's get started...

DAY 1:
THE DICHOTOMY OF CONTROL

"You have power over your mind - not outside events. Realize this, and you will find strength."
- Marcus Aurelius

In the pursuit of a happy life, we must recognize that much of what we encounter is beyond our influence.

Today, we begin our Stoic journey by contemplating what is within our control.

Stoic Affirmation for today:
"I focus on what lies within my control—my thoughts and actions. I release attachment to outcomes beyond my power."

Stoic Meditation: Reflect on situations in your life where you've felt distressed due to circumstances beyond your control. How can embracing this dichotomy lead you to greater inner peace and happiness?

DAY 2: ACCEPTING EXTERNAL EVENTS

"Accept the things to which fate binds you, and love the people with whom fate brings you together, but do so with all your heart."

\- Marcus Aurelius, Meditations

Marcus Aurelius reminds us to embrace life's experiences and the people we meet along the way. Acceptance doesn't mean passivity; it's about engaging fully with what life presents, without resistance.

Stoic Affirmation for today:

"I accept life's events and people as they are, engaging with them wholeheartedly without wishing them to be otherwise."

Stoic Meditation:

Think about a recent event or interaction that you resisted or wished was different. How might fully accepting and engaging with it change your perspective on or feelings about it?

DAY 3:
INNER FREEDOM

"He who fears death will never do anything worthy of a man who is alive."

- Marcus Aurelius, Meditations 4:19

This meditation by Marcus Aurelius invites us to confront one of our greatest fears - death - and in doing so, find freedom.

By facing our fears, we liberate ourselves from them, allowing us to live fully and with purpose.

Stoic Affirmation for today:

"In facing my fears, I find strength and freedom. I choose to live boldly, unshackled by fear of the end."

Stoic Meditation:

Consider an action or decision you've been avoiding due to fear. How can confronting this fear directly enhance your sense of freedom and vitality in life?

DAY 4:
THE POWER OF PERCEPTION

"Everything we hear is an opinion, not a fact. Everything we see is a perspective, not the truth."
- Marcus Aurelius, Meditations 12:18

Marcus Aurelius teaches us about the subjectivity of our perceptions. What we consider truth is often colored by our personal views and beliefs.

Recognizing this can free us from rigid thinking and open us to a more flexible and understanding approach to life.

Stoic Affirmation for today:
"I acknowledge that my perspective is just one of many. I remain open and adaptable to new information and viewpoints."

Stoic Meditation:
Reflect on a recent disagreement or misunderstanding. How might acknowledging the subjectivity of your own and others' perceptions change how you approach such situations in the future?

DAY 5:
TAKING ACTION WITHIN OUR POWER

"You have power over your mind – not outside events. Realize this, and you will find strength."
- Marcus Aurelius, Meditations 6:41

Marcus Aurelius highlights the importance of focusing on areas within our control — our thoughts, attitudes, and actions.

By concentrating on these, we empower ourselves to create positive change and maintain inner tranquility, regardless of external circumstances.

Stoic Affirmation for today:

"I direct my energy towards what I can change, finding strength and serenity in my ability to shape my own actions and attitudes."

Stoic Meditation:

Think about a situation where you felt powerless. How can shifting your focus to aspects within your control empower you in similar situations in the future?

DAY 6:
RESPONDING TO OTHERS

"When another blames you or hates you, or people voice similar criticisms, go to their souls, penetrate inside and see what sort of people they are. You will realize that there is no need to be racked with anxiety that they should hold any particular opinion about you."

- Marcus Aurelius, Meditations 9:18

Marcus Aurelius advises us to look beyond surface criticisms and understand the perspective of others. By doing so, we can respond to criticism with empathy and detachment, maintaining our inner peace and not allowing others' opinions to disturb us.

Stoic Affirmation for today:

"I approach criticism with empathy and understanding, not allowing it to disturb my inner peace or self-worth."

Stoic Meditation:

Recall a recent instance where you were criticized. How can understanding the critic's perspective help you respond more thoughtfully and maintain your composure?

DAY 7:
WEEKLY REFLECTION ON CONTROL

As we conclude this week, we reflect on the Stoic teachings about control.

Marcus Aurelius reminds us that true power lies in controlling our mind and reactions, not in altering external events.

Stoic Affirmation for today:

"I reflect on my week with mindfulness, recognizing areas where I practiced control over my thoughts and actions, and areas where I can improve."

Stoic Meditation:

Take time today to journal about your experiences this week.

How have the concepts discussed influenced your actions and reactions?

What lessons have you learned about what you can control and what you cannot?

DAY 8:

PEACE AMIDST CHAOS

Amidst life's chaos, Marcus Aurelius counsels us to be steadfast and unshaken.

Like a cliff against the sea, we can face life's tumult with calmness and resilience, not allowing external chaos to disturb our inner peace.

Stoic Affirmation for today:
"In the midst of chaos, I stand firm and calm, not swayed by external events but maintaining my inner peace."

Stoic Meditation:
Reflect on a chaotic or stressful situation in your life. How can you embody the steadiness of a promontory in this scenario, maintaining your serenity and resilience?

DAY 9:
SERENITY IN THE SELF

- Marcus Aurelius, Meditations 4:3

Marcus Aurelius reminds us of the sanctuary that exists within ourselves.

When the world outside is turbulent, we can always turn inward to find peace and serenity.

This inner refuge is always available, a place of calm and stability amidst any storm.

Stoic Affirmation for today:

"I carry a sanctuary within me. In moments of external turmoil, I turn inward to find peace and clarity."

Stoic Meditation:

Consider a moment when you felt overwhelmed by external circumstances. How might turning inward and seeking serenity in your own soul change your response to or perception of these events?

DAY 10:
MANAGING ANGER

"How much more grievous are the consequences of anger than the causes of it."
- Marcus Aurelius, Meditations 11:18

Marcus Aurelius advises us on the destructive nature of anger. Often, the aftermath of anger is far worse than the event that triggered it. Recognizing this can help us manage our responses and choose a more constructive path when faced with frustration or provocation.

Stoic Affirmation for today:

"I choose to respond to provocation with calmness and understanding, knowing that anger often brings more harm than good."

Stoic Meditation:

Recall a recent situation where you felt angry. Reflect on how this anger affected you and others. How might a calm and measured response have led to a better outcome?

DAY 11: OVERCOMING DISTURBANCES

Here, Marcus Aurelius teaches us about the power of perception in shaping our reactions to external events. Our disturbances are often self-created through our interpretations and attitudes.

By changing our perspective, we can alleviate our distress and maintain our composure.

Stoic Affirmation for today:

"I control my reactions to external events. I choose perspectives that bring peace and equanimity."

Stoic Meditation:

Identify a recent situation that disturbed you. How might altering your perspective on this event change your emotional response to it?

DAY 12:
THE ROLE OF EGO

"Whenever you are about to find fault with someone, ask yourself the following question: What fault of mine most nearly resembles the one I am about to criticize?"
- Marcus Aurelius, Meditations 10:30

Aurelius prompts us to reflect on our own faults before judging others, highlighting the role of ego in our perceptions and interactions. This introspection fosters humility and empathy, reducing conflicts and misunderstandings.

Stoic Affirmation for today:

"Before I judge others, I look within myself. My focus is on self-improvement, not fault-finding."

Stoic Meditation:

Think of a recent time you criticized someone. How does reflecting on your own similar faults change your view of that person and situation?

DAY 13:
FINDING CALM

"A real man doesn't give way to anger and discontent, and such a person has strength, courage, and endurance—unlike the angry and complaining. The nearer a man comes to a calm mind, the closer he is to strength."
- Marcus Aurelius, Meditations 11:18.7

Aurelius suggests that true strength lies in maintaining calm and composure, not in giving in to anger.

Cultivating a calm mind equips us with the resilience to face life's challenges effectively.

Stoic Affirmation for today:
"My strength is in my calmness. I choose to respond to life's challenges with serenity and understanding."

Stoic Meditation:
Reflect on a recent stressful situation. How could maintaining calm have changed the outcome or your experience of the event?

DAY 14:
WEEKLY REFLECTION ON PEACE

As we conclude a week focused on cultivating inner peace, Marcus Aurelius reminds us to be understanding and patient with others while holding ourselves to high standards.

This balance is essential for maintaining tranquility and harmony in our lives.

Stoic Affirmation for today:

"I practice patience and tolerance with others, while striving for personal excellence and self-discipline."

Stoic Meditation:

Reflect on your week: How did you practice patience with others? In what ways were you strict with yourself? How have these practices contributed to your sense of peace?

DAY 15:
THE NATURE OF CHANGE

"Time is a river, a violent current of events, glimpsed once and already carried past us, and another follows and is gone."
- Marcus Aurelius, Meditations 4:43

Marcus Aurelius compares time to a swiftly flowing river, emphasizing the constant and unstoppable nature of change.

This perspective encourages us to embrace the present and understand the transient nature of life's events, both joyful and challenging.

Stoic Affirmation for today:
"I embrace the flow of life, understanding that change is constant and inevitable. I remain adaptable and open to the present moment."

Stoic Meditation:
Consider an aspect of your life that is changing or has recently changed. How can embracing the nature of this change enhance your adaptability toward and appreciation of the present?

DAY 16: IMPERMANENCE OF POSSESSIONS

"Very little is needed to make a happy life; it is all within yourself, in your way of thinking."

- Marcus Aurelius, Meditations 7:67

Marcus Aurelius reminds us of the impermanence and insubstantial nature of material possessions.

True happiness comes not from external acquisitions, but from our internal perspective and contentment with what we have.

Stoic Affirmation for today:

"I find joy and fulfillment not in possessions, but in my thoughts, relationships, and experiences. My happiness is independent of material wealth."

Stoic Meditation:

Reflect on a time when you sought happiness in material things. How did this compare to the joy found in intangible aspects of your life, like relationships or personal achievements?

DAY 17:
LIFE'S TRANSITIONS

"Loss is nothing else but change,
and change is Nature's delight."
- Marcus Aurelius, Meditations 4:35.1

Marcus Aurelius presents change, even in the form of loss, as a natural and positive aspect of life.

Life's transitions, whether they bring joy or sorrow, are part of the universe's constant rhythm.

Embracing transitions as natural helps us navigate life with grace and resilience.

Stoic Affirmation for today:

"I accept and embrace life's transitions, understanding them as natural and essential parts of my growth and experience."

Stoic Meditation:

Think about a significant change you've recently experienced. How does viewing this change as a natural and positive part of life alter your perception of and emotional response to it?

DAY 18:
EMBRACING MORTALITY

"Think of yourself as dead.
You have lived your life.
Now take what's left and live it properly."
- Marcus Aurelius, Meditations 7:56

Marcus Aurelius urges us to confront our mortality to fully appreciate and utilize the time we have.

By embracing the inevitability of death, we can live more purposefully, valuing each moment and focusing on what truly matters.

Stoic Affirmation for today:
"Aware of my mortality, I live each day with purpose, cherishing each moment and focusing on what truly enriches my life."

Stoic Meditation:
Consider how the awareness of your mortality might influence your daily choices and actions. How can this perspective help you live more intentionally and meaningfully?

DAY 19:
GROWTH AND DECAY

"All things are in a state of flux and growth, and decay is but a component of creation and recreation."
- Marcus Aurelius, Meditations 6:36

In this meditation, Marcus Aurelius reminds us that growth and decay are natural and continuous processes in life.

Understanding this cycle helps us accept change and loss as necessary for new beginnings and growth, rather than as purely negative events.

Stoic Affirmation for today:

"I embrace the natural cycle of growth and decay, understanding that each ending paves the way for new beginnings and opportunities."

Stoic Meditation:

Reflect on an aspect of your life that has ended or changed significantly. How can this perspective of growth and decay help you see this change as an opportunity for new growth?

DAY 20:
LETTING GO

"Leave behind the past and the future.
Live in the present."
- Marcus Aurelius, Meditations 7:29

Marcus Aurelius emphasizes the importance of letting go of past regrets and future anxieties to fully embrace the present.

This focus on the here and now allows us to live more fully, engage more deeply with our current experiences, and find contentment.

Stoic Affirmation for today:

"I release my hold on the past and my worries about the future, choosing instead to live fully in the present moment."

Stoic Meditation:

Consider a past regret or future worry that occupies your mind. How can letting go of these thoughts help you engage more fully with the present?

DAY 21:
WEEKLY REFLECTION ON CHANGE

"Time is like a river made up of the events which happen, and a violent stream; for as soon as a thing has been seen, it is carried away, and another comes in its place, and this will be carried away too."
- Marcus Aurelius, Meditations 4:43

As we reflect on this week's focus on change, Marcus Aurelius's words remind us of the constant flow of time and events.

Embracing this continual flux helps us adapt and find peace amid life's inevitable transformations.

Stoic Affirmation for today:
"I reflect on the changes I've experienced this week, learning to flow with them like a river, embracing each moment as it comes and goes."

Stoic Meditation:
Look back over the past week. How did you respond to change? How can you apply the lessons of impermanence and flux to upcoming changes in your life?

DAY 22:
DEFINING WISDOM

"The best revenge is to be unlike him
who performed the injustice."
- Marcus Aurelius, Meditations 6:6

Marcus Aurelius offers a profound insight into wisdom — it's not just about knowledge, but also about character.

True wisdom involves choosing a path of integrity and virtue, especially when faced with wrongdoing. It's about being better, not just knowing more.

Stoic Affirmation for today:
"In the face of injustice, I choose the path of wisdom, acting with integrity and virtue, rather than seeking revenge or mirroring negative behaviors."

Stoic Meditation:
Reflect on a situation where you felt wronged. How can applying wisdom and integrity, rather than retaliation, lead to a more positive outcome for your personal growth?

DAY 23:
THE WISE MINDSET

"You have power over your mind — not outside events.
Realize this, and you will find strength."
- Marcus Aurelius, Meditations 6:41

This meditation from Marcus Aurelius highlights the essence of a wise mindset: recognizing that our power lies in how we perceive and respond to external events, not in the events themselves.

This understanding is the cornerstone of resilience, inner peace, and strength.

Stoic Affirmation for today:
"I cultivate strength through my wise mindset, understanding that my power lies in my reactions and perceptions, not in external circumstances."

Stoic Meditation:
Consider a recent event that you reacted strongly to. How might a shift in your mindset affect your perception of and response to similar events in the future?

DAY 24:
LEARNING FROM OTHERS

"Take a good hard look at people's ruling principle, especially of the wise, what they run away from and what they seek out."
- Marcus Aurelius, Meditations 4:38

Marcus Aurelius encourages us to observe and learn from the wisdom of others.

By understanding what drives the choices and actions of wise individuals, we can gain insights into virtuous living and apply these lessons to our own lives.

Stoic Affirmation for today:

"I seek to learn from the wisdom of others, observing their virtues and incorporating their valuable lessons into my own journey towards self-improvement."

Stoic Meditation:

Reflect on someone you consider wise. What are their guiding principles? How can their approach to life inspire or inform your own actions and decisions?

DAY 25:
KNOWLEDGE VS. WISDOM

"Not to assume it's impossible because you find it hard. But to recognize that if it's humanly possible, you can do it too."
- Marcus Aurelius, Meditations 6:19

Marcus Aurelius differentiates between mere knowledge and true wisdom here.

Knowledge might tell us about the difficulty of a task, but wisdom inspires the understanding that what is possible for others is possible for us as well.

It's a call to action, grounded in the belief in our own potential.

Stoic Affirmation for today:

"I embrace challenges, knowing that wisdom lies in the effort and belief in my own capabilities, beyond mere understanding."

Stoic Meditation:

Think of a challenge you initially thought impossible. How can this perspective of wisdom guide you in approaching and overcoming this challenge?

DAY 26:
THE PHILOSOPHER KING

Marcus Aurelius, often regarded as the philosopher king, emphasizes the importance of living by principles of truth and righteousness.

His guidance reflects the Stoic ideal that one's actions and words should always align with moral and ethical integrity.

Stoic Affirmation for today:

"I commit to actions and words that reflect truth and righteousness, embodying the principles of the philosopher king in my daily life."

Stoic Meditation:

Reflect on recent decisions or conversations. Were your actions and words aligned with your true values and principles? How can you more fully embody these ideals in your everyday life?

DAY 27:
THE FOLLY OF IGNORANCE

"It is not death that a man should fear, but he should fear never beginning to live."
\- Marcus Aurelius, Meditations 7:13

In this passage, Marcus Aurelius points out that the true misfortune is not death itself, but living a life clouded by ignorance and missed opportunities.

Wisdom calls for embracing life fully, with an open heart and mind, rather than retreating into the shadows of ignorance and fear.

Stoic Affirmation for today:

"I embrace the fullness of life, seeking knowledge and experience over the comfort of ignorance, and living each day with purpose and openness."

Stoic Meditation:

Reflect on an area of your life where fear or ignorance has held you back. How can embracing knowledge and experience help you start truly living in this area?

DAY 28:
WEEKLY REFLECTION ON WISDOM

---

*"Look back over the past,
with its changing empires that rose and fell,
and you can foresee the future too."*
- Marcus Aurelius, Meditations 7:49

As we conclude a week focused on wisdom, Marcus Aurelius encourages us to reflect on the past to gain insights into the future.

This week's journey has been about understanding the difference between knowledge and wisdom, learning from others, and embracing the principles of living wisely.

Stoic Affirmation for today:
"I reflect on my past experiences as lessons for the future, understanding that wisdom grows from both success and failure."

Stoic Meditation:
Reflect on your week: How have you applied wisdom in your daily life? What lessons have you learned, and how can they guide your future decisions and actions?

DAY 29:
VIRTUE AS A GOOD

"Just that you do the right thing. The rest doesn't matter."
- Marcus Aurelius, Meditations 6:2

Marcus Aurelius succinctly captures the essence of Stoic philosophy here: the highest good lies in virtuous action.

It's not about external recognition or reward, but the intrinsic value of doing what is right and moral.

Stoic Affirmation for today:
"My focus is on acting virtuously in all situations. The true reward lies in the action itself, not in external outcomes."

Stoic Meditation:
Think about a recent decision you made. Was it guided by virtue? How did it feel to act in alignment with your moral principles, regardless of the outcome?

DAY 30:
HONESTY AND INTEGRITY

---

*"Waste no more time arguing what
a good man should be. Be one."*
- Marcus Aurelius, Meditations 10:16

In this powerful statement, Marcus Aurelius calls us to embody the virtues of honesty and integrity. It's not enough to merely discuss or admire these qualities; we must actively live by them in our daily interactions and decisions.

Stoic Affirmation for today:

"I commit to being a person of honesty and integrity, letting my actions speak louder than words in demonstrating these virtues."

Stoic Meditation:

Reflect on your day: Where did you have the opportunity to practice honesty and integrity? How did it impact your sense of self and your interactions with others?

DAY 31: COURAGE IN DAILY LIFE

"Do not be ashamed to be helped; for it is your business to do your duty like a soldier in the assault on a town. How then, if being lame you cannot mount up on the battlements alone, but with the help of another it is possible?"
- Marcus Aurelius, Meditations 7:7

Marcus Aurelius highlights the virtue of courage, not just in grand acts, but in everyday life, including seeking help when needed. Courage in daily life often means acknowledging our limitations and being open to assistance, as well as facing everyday challenges with resilience.

Stoic Affirmation for today:

"I exhibit courage daily, not only in facing challenges but also in acknowledging my needs and seeking help when necessary."

Stoic Meditation:

Consider a situation where you may have hesitated to ask for help. How can embracing courage in its various forms enhance your ability to handle such situations in the future?

DAY 32:
JUSTICE AND FAIRNESS

Marcus Aurelius here speaks to the heart of justice and fairness: maintaining integrity and honoring commitments, even when it might bring personal disadvantage.

True justice involves upholding ethical standards and treating others with respect and fairness, regardless of the situation.

Stoic Affirmation for today:

"I hold fast to my principles of justice and fairness, knowing that my integrity is more valuable than any short-term gain."

Stoic Meditation:

Reflect on a recent decision where you faced a conflict between self-interest and doing what was right. How did you respond, and what does this say about your commitment to justice and fairness?

DAY 33: SELF-DISCIPLINE AND TEMPERANCE

"It is in your power to withdraw yourself whenever you desire. Perfect tranquility within consists in the good ordering of the mind, the realm of your own."
- Marcus Aurelius, Meditations 4:3

Marcus Aurelius emphasizes the importance of self-discipline and temperance for inner peace. These virtues are about controlling our impulses and desires, leading to a well-ordered mind and a balanced life.

Practicing self-discipline and temperance is essential for maintaining tranquility and focus.

Stoic Affirmation for today:
"I exercise self-discipline and temperance in my thoughts and actions, understanding that true peace comes from a well-ordered and balanced mind."

Stoic Meditation:
Think of a moment when you successfully exercised self-discipline

or temperance. How did this contribute to your sense of inner peace
and balance?

DAY 34:
HUMLITY AND MODESTY

"It never ceases to amaze me: we all love ourselves more than other people, but care more about their opinion than our own."
- Marcus Aurelius, Meditations 12:4

In this reflection, Marcus Aurelius points to the paradox of valuing others' opinions over our assessment of ourselves.

He suggests a need for humility and modesty, virtues that involve a realistic view of our own importance and an openness to learn from others, free from the trap of external validation.

Stoic Affirmation for today:
"I embrace humility and modesty, valuing my own worth, while remaining open to the wisdom and perspectives of others."

Stoic Meditation:
Consider a recent situation where you were overly concerned with someone else's opinion. How can practicing humility and modesty change your approach to similar situations in the future?

DAY 35:
WEEKLY REFLECTION ON VIRTUE

"What is not good for the swarm is not good for the bee."
- Marcus Aurelius, Meditations 6:54

As we conclude this week's focus on virtue, Marcus Aurelius reminds us of the interconnectedness of our actions and their impact on the larger community.

This reflection week has been about understanding and practicing the core Stoic virtues: honesty, courage, justice, self-discipline, and humility, and recognizing their role in both personal growth and societal well-being.

Stoic Affirmation for today:

"I reflect on the virtues I have practiced this week, understanding how they contribute not only to my personal development but also to the greater good."

Stoic Meditation:

Reflect on your week: How did you embody these virtues in your daily life? How did practicing these virtues impact your interactions and your community?

DAY 36:
THE ROLE OF ADVERSITY

"The impediment to action advances action. What stands in the way becomes the way."
- Marcus Aurelius, Meditations 5:20

Marcus Aurelius presents adversity not as a barrier, but as a catalyst for growth and action.

Challenges and obstacles are opportunities to demonstrate our resilience and adaptability, to strengthen our character, and to advance our goals in unexpected ways.

Stoic Affirmation for today:

"I view each obstacle as an opportunity to grow and advance. Adversity strengthens my resolve and sharpens my abilities."

Stoic Meditation:

Think about a recent challenge or obstacle. How can this perspective transform your approach to adversity, turning obstacles into pathways for growth and achievement?

DAY 37: PERSEVERANCE

"Concentrate every minute like a Roman—like a man—on doing what's in front of you with precise and genuine seriousness, tenderly, willingly, with justice."
- Marcus Aurelius, Meditations 2:5

Marcus Aurelius encourages us to approach our tasks and challenges with dedication and focus, embodying the spirit of perseverance.

By giving our full attention to the present moment and task, we cultivate a mindset of resilience and determination.

Stoic Affirmation for today:

"I approach my tasks with focus and dedication, persisting with seriousness and integrity, as if each task were my last."

Stoic Meditation:

Reflect on a task or goal that requires your perseverance. How can focusing intently on the present moment and action strengthen your resolve and aid in overcoming challenges?

DAY 38:
OVERCOMING OBSTACLES

"Our actions may be impeded, but there can be no impeding our intentions or dispositions. Because we can accommodate and adapt. The mind adapts and converts to its own purposes the obstacle to our acting."
- Marcus Aurelius, Meditations 5:20

Marcus Aurelius highlights the power of the mind to transform obstacles into opportunities.

When faced with challenges, our mindset and adaptability determine our success.
By reorienting our approach and perspective, we can find new ways to achieve our goals.

Stoic Affirmation for today:

"I adapt and transform obstacles into stepping-stones for success."

Stoic Meditation:

Consider a current obstacle in your life. How can a shift in perspective or approach turn this challenge into an opportunity for growth or innovation?

DAY 39:
LESSONS IN FAILURE

Marcus Aurelius reminds us that, in times of failure, our strength lies in our response and mindset. Failure is not a defeat but an opportunity to learn, grow, and fortify our resilience.

Our reaction to failure defines our path forward more than the failure itself.

Stoic Affirmation for today:

"In every failure, I seek the lesson and opportunity for growth. Every lesson I learn shapes my path to success."

Stoic Meditation:

Reflect on a recent failure. What lessons can you learn from this experience, and how can these insights strengthen your future endeavors?

DAY 40:
STOIC TOUGHNESS

"Be like the headland, on which the waves break constantly, which still stands firm, while the foaming waters are put to rest around it."

— Marcus Aurelius, Meditations 4:49

Marcus Aurelius uses the metaphor of a headland facing unrelenting waves to illustrate Stoic toughness.

It's about being resilient and unwavering in the face of life's challenges and adversities.

This toughness isn't about being unfeeling or harsh, but about maintaining inner strength and calmness amidst external turmoil.

Stoic Affirmation for today:

"I stand firm like a headland against the waves. No matter the challenges, I maintain my inner strength and composure."

Stoic Meditation:

Reflect on a situation in your life that tests your resilience. How can adopting the steadfastness of a headland provide you with the strength to endure and prevail?

DAY 41: RECOVERY AND REJUVENATION

Stoicism isn't just about enduring hardship; it's also about recognizing the need for rest and rejuvenation. Neglecting self-care and recovery can be an injustice to ourselves.

By allowing ourselves time to recharge our batteries, we're better equipped to face life's challenges with renewed strength and clarity.

Stoic Affirmation for today:

"I allow myself time to rest and recover, understanding this is essential for sustained resilience and strength."

Stoic Meditation:

Think about how you approach your own rest and rejuvenation. How can integrating intentional rest enhance your ability to face future challenges?

DAY 42:
WEEKLY REFLECTION ON RESILIENCE

"Constantly regard the universe as one living being, having one substance and one soul; and observe how all things have reference to one perception, the perception of this one living being."
- Marcus Aurelius, Meditations 4:40

As we reflect on this week's focus on resilience, Marcus Aurelius reminds us of the interconnectedness of all things and the importance of considering our part in the larger context of life.

Stoic Affirmation for today:

"I choose both strength in adversity and to accept failure as a teacher, rather than the final end."

Stoic Meditation:

Reflect on your experiences of resilience this past week. How did you face challenges, and how did you allow yourself time for recovery? How can these insights guide your approach to resilience in the future?

DAY 43:
THE GIFT OF LIFE

Marcus Aurelius encourages us to start each day with gratitude for the simple yet profound gift of life itself.

Recognizing the value of every moment we're alive, and the opportunities that present themselves for thought, enjoyment, and love, can profoundly shift our perspective and approach to the day.

Stoic Affirmation for today:
"Each day, I cherish the gift of life, embracing each moment with gratitude and an open heart."

Stoic Meditation:
As you start your day, reflect on the simple privileges of being alive. How does this perspective influence your feelings and actions throughout the day?

DAY 44:
APPRECIATING THE PRESENT

"Concentrate on the present."
- Marcus Aurelius, Meditations 8:22

Marcus Aurelius reminds us of the importance of living in the now. The present moment holds the key to a fulfilling life, free from the distractions of past regrets and future anxieties.

Stoic Affirmation for today:

"I focus on the present, finding joy and purpose in the here and now."

Stoic Meditation:

Reflect on how being present can enrich your experiences today.

DAY 45: THE SIMPLE JOYS

Marcus Aurelius reminds us of the beauty in simplicity. True happiness often lies in appreciating small, everyday joys.

Stoic Affirmation for today:
"I find contentment in life's simple pleasures, recognizing their profound impact on my happiness."

Stoic Meditation:
Today, identify and savor a simple joy in your life. What is it and how does it enhance your experience of life?

DAY 46:
VALUING RELATIONSHIPS

"People exist for the sake of one another. Teach them or bear with them."

\- Marcus Aurelius, Meditations 8:59

Marcus Aurelius highlights the significance of relationships and our interdependence. Our interactions can be opportunities for teaching, learning, and patience.

Stoic Affirmation for today:

"I value my relationships, seeing them as opportunities for mutual growth and understanding."

Stoic Meditation:

Reflect on how you can contribute positively to your relationships today.

DAY 47:
GRATITUDE IN HARDSHIP

"The art of living is more like wrestling than dancing."
- Marcus Aurelius, Meditations 7:61

This analogy by Marcus Aurelius suggests that life requires active engagement, resilience, and adaptability, much like wrestling.

Even in hardship, there are lessons to be learned and strengths to be gained.

Stoic Affirmation for today:

"In every hardship, I find strength and lessons to be grateful for. My challenges are opportunities for growth."

Stoic Meditation:

Consider a recent difficulty. What can you be grateful for in this challenge and what strength can you gain from it?

DAY 48:
THE WEALTH OF GRATITUDE

"Gratitude is not only the greatest of virtues but the parent of all others."

- Marcus Aurelius, Meditations 7:67

Marcus Aurelius emphasizes the foundational role of gratitude.

Acknowledging and appreciating the good in our lives can enrich our experiences and relationships, fostering a wealth of positive emotions and virtues.

Stoic Affirmation for today:

"I cultivate a deep sense of gratitude, recognizing it as the source of true wealth and well-being in my life."

Stoic Meditation:

Reflect on three aspects of your life you are deeply grateful for today.

DAY 49:
WEEKLY REFLECTION ON GRATITUDE

"Look back on the past and remember how merciful the gods have been to you."

- Marcus Aurelius, Meditations 10:8

Ending the week on gratitude, Marcus Aurelius prompts us to reflect on life's blessings.

Recognizing the good, even in small measures, builds a foundation of contentment and appreciation.

Stoic Affirmation for today:

"I reflect on my week with gratitude, appreciating the kindnesses, moments of joy, and lessons learned."

Stoic Meditation:

Identify five positive things from this week you are thankful for. How have these moments shaped your perspective and feelings?

DAY 50:
DEFINING HAPPINESS

"The happiness of your life depends upon the quality of your thoughts."

- Marcus Aurelius, Meditations 4:39

Marcus Aurelius suggests that happiness is not derived from external circumstances, but from the way we process and perceive the world.

Our thoughts and attitudes are the architects of our happiness.

Stoic Affirmation for today:

"I cultivate positive, constructive thoughts, understanding that they are the foundation of my happiness."

Stoic Meditation:

Reflect on how your thoughts influence your sense of happiness. How can you foster more positive and beneficial thinking?

DAY 51:
THE STOIC JOY

Marcus Aurelius encourages finding joy in acceptance and love for our current life and companions.

Stoic joy comes from embracing and valuing our present circumstances and relationships.

Stoic Affirmation for today:

"I find joy in acceptance, cherishing my life as it is and the people in it."

Stoic Meditation:

Today, consider how acceptance of your current circumstances can lead to a deeper sense of joy and contentment.

DAY 52:
PLEASURE VS.
CONTENTMENT

"Wealth consists not in having great possessions, but in having few wants."
- Marcus Aurelius, Meditations 7:33

Here, Marcus Aurelius differentiates between fleeting pleasures and true contentment.

While pleasures can be temporary and external, contentment comes from within, through appreciating what we have and minimizing desires.

Unlike some types of pleasure, contentment is never an evil.

Stoic Affirmation for today:
"I seek contentment over temporary pleasures, understanding that true happiness lies in simplicity and appreciation."

Stoic Meditation:
Reflect on the difference between a recent pleasure and a moment of contentment. How do these experiences affect your lasting sense of happiness?

DAY 53:
THE INTERNAL SOURCE OF HAPPINESS

"No man is happy who does not think himself so."
- Marcus Aurelius, Meditations 4:11

Marcus Aurelius reminds us that happiness is an internal state, shaped by our thoughts and perceptions.

It is not external circumstances, but our internal dialogue and attitude that determine our happiness.

Stoic Affirmation for today:
"I cultivate positive and constructive thoughts, recognizing they are the keys to my inner happiness."

Stoic Meditation:
Today, focus on how your thoughts influence your mood and outlook. What changes can you make to foster a more positive internal environment?

DAY 54:
REMOVING DESIRES

Marcus Aurelius suggests that tranquility and contentment come from focusing on what is truly essential, rather than being driven by endless desires.

Simplifying life to its essentials can lead to greater peace and satisfaction.

Stoic Affirmation for today:

"I focus on what is essential and let go of unnecessary desires. This simplicity brings tranquility to my life."

Stoic Meditation:

Think about areas of your life where reducing desires and simplifying things could lead to more peace and contentment.

DAY 55:
THE STOIC AND SOCIETY

"What injures the hive, injures the bee."
- Marcus Aurelius, Meditations 6:54

Marcus Aurelius reminds us of our interconnectedness with society.

The well-being of the community affects the individual, just as the actions of the individual impact the community.

As Stoics, we are encouraged to act in ways that benefit the greater good.

Stoic Affirmation for today:
"I act mindfully, knowing my choices and actions contribute to the welfare of my community and, in turn, to my own well-being."

Stoic Meditation:
Reflect on how your actions impact those around you. How can you contribute positively to your community today?

DAY 56:
WEEKLY REFLECTION ON HAPPINESS

As we conclude our week focusing on happiness, Marcus Aurelius inspires us to find joy in the world around us.

This week has been about understanding happiness as an internal state, influenced by our thoughts, actions, and how we choose to view our experiences.

Stoic Affirmation for today:
"I am thankful for the moments of happiness I experienced this week, recognizing their source in my thoughts and perspectives."

Stoic Meditation:
Reflect on how your internal state has affected your happiness this week. What thoughts or actions led to moments of joy and contentment?

DAY 57:
THE SOCIAL ANIMAL

"Human beings are social animals, born for one another's sake."
- Marcus Aurelius, Meditations 8:12

Marcus Aurelius reminds us of our inherent social nature.

We are intrinsically linked to one another, and our interactions and relationships form a fundamental part of our existence and well-being.

Stoic Affirmation for today:
"I embrace my role as a social being, understanding that my connections with others are essential to both my well-being and theirs."

Stoic Meditation:
Today, consider how your social interactions contribute to your life. How can you strengthen and positively engage in these relationships?

DAY 58: KINDNESS AND COMPASSION

"Kindness is invincible, provided it's sincere—not ironic or an act. What can even the most vicious person do if you keep treating him with kindness and gently set him straight?"
- Marcus Aurelius, Meditations 11:18.9

Marcus Aurelius encourages a balance of kindness and self-discipline. Showing compassion and understanding to others while holding ourselves to high standards of personal conduct is essential for a harmonious life.

Stoic Affirmation for today:
"I practice kindness and compassion towards others while maintaining self-discipline and personal growth."

Stoic Meditation:
Reflect on how you can show more kindness and compassion in your interactions today, while also being mindful of your personal responsibilities and growth.

DAY 59:
DEALING WITH DIFFICULT PEOPLE

"To feel affection for people even when they make mistakes is uniquely human. You can do it if you simply recognize: that they're human too, that they act out of ignorance, against their will, and that you'll both be dead before long."
- Marcus Aurelius, Meditations 7:22

Marcus Aurelius advises us to approach difficult people with empathy and understanding.

Recognizing our shared humanity and the limitations of human nature can help us respond with patience and compassion.

Stoic Affirmation for today:
"I approach difficult people with empathy and patience, understanding our shared humanity and imperfections."

Stoic Meditation:
Consider a challenging person in your life. How can this perspective of shared humanity and imperfection change your interactions with them?

DAY 60:
FORGIVENESS

"The best way of avenging thyself is not to become like the wrong-doer."

- Marcus Aurelius, Meditations 6:6

Marcus Aurelius points out that true forgiveness lies in maintaining our own integrity and virtue, rather than mirroring the wrongdoer.

Forgiveness is a personal strength, a release from the burden of resentment, and a step towards inner peace.

Stoic Affirmation for today:

"I choose forgiveness, understanding it as a path to personal peace and integrity, rather than a concession to those who have wronged me."

Stoic Meditation:

Think about a situation where forgiveness might be challenging yet healing. How can practicing forgiveness improve your well-being and peace of mind?

DAY 61:
THE COMMUNITY AND THE INDIVIDUAL

"All things are linked with one another, and this oneness is sacred; there is nothing that is not interconnected with everything else."
- Marcus Aurelius, Meditations 6:38

Marcus Aurelius speaks to the deep interconnectedness between the individual and the community.

Our actions and well-being are intrinsically linked to the larger whole.

Stoic Affirmation for today:
"I recognize my connection with the community and strive to contribute positively, understanding our shared existence and interdependence."

Stoic Meditation:
Reflect on how your actions impact your community and vice versa. How can you enhance this mutual relationship for the greater good?

DAY 62:
LOVE AND STOICISM

"Love the humankind. Follow the divine."
- Marcus Aurelius, Meditations 9:31

Marcus Aurelius encourages a universal love for humanity, aligning with Stoic principles that emphasize virtue and the greater good.

This love is not merely an emotion but an action — a commitment to treat others with kindness, respect, and understanding, reflecting our shared humanity.

Stoic Affirmation for today:

"I practice love in my daily interactions, treating others with kindness, empathy, and respect, as part of my commitment to virtue and the greater good."

Stoic Meditation:

Think about ways you can express this universal love in your daily life. How can your actions today reflect a deep respect and care for those around you?

DAY 63:
WEEKLY REFLECTION ON RELATIONSHIPS

As we conclude our week focusing on relationships, Marcus Aurelius reminds us of the fleeting nature of life and the importance of making the most of our current relationships.

Reflecting thoughtfully and acting justly in our interactions can deepen our connections and enhance our experiences.

Stoic Affirmation for today:
"I reflect on the relationships I've nurtured this week, valuing each moment and interaction for the unique role they play in my life."

Stoic Meditation:
Consider the relationships you've focused on this week. How have they impacted your life, and how have you contributed to their growth and richness?

DAY 64:
THE VALUE OF LABOR

"Labor willingly and diligently, undistracted and aware of the common interest."
- Marcus Aurelius, Meditations 6:7

Marcus Aurelius emphasizes the value of labor, not just as a means to an end, but as a purposeful and mindful activity that contributes to the greater good.

Work done with dedication and awareness is both personally fulfilling and beneficial to the community.

Stoic Affirmation for today:

"I approach my work with diligence and purpose, understanding its value in my personal growth and its contribution to the wider world."

Stoic Meditation:

Reflect on how your work can be approached as a meaningful contribution, not just a task. How does this perspective change your approach to labor today?

DAY 65:
DUTY AND DISCIPLINE

"Do every act of your life as though it were the very last act of your life."

- Marcus Aurelius, Meditations 2:5

Marcus Aurelius reminds us of the importance of duty and discipline in our actions.

Treating each task as if it were our last ensures mindfulness and commitment.

Stoic Affirmation for today:

"I perform each duty with utmost discipline and care, as if it were my final act."

Stoic Meditation:

Today, how can treating each task with such significance influence your diligence and commitment?

DAY 66:
WORK AS A FORM OF VIRTUE

"Waste no more time arguing what a good man should be. Be one."

- Marcus Aurelius, Meditations 10:16

This guidance from Marcus Aurelius encourages us to embody virtue through action, including our work.

Our daily tasks and responsibilities are opportunities to practice virtues like diligence, integrity, and service.

Stoic Affirmation for today:

"My work is an expression of virtue. I commit to integrity, diligence, and excellence in my tasks."

Stoic Meditation:

Reflect on how your work can serve as a medium for practicing and expressing your virtues today.

DAY 67:
PROFESSIONAL CHALLENGES

"The mind adapts and converts to its own purposes the obstacle to our acting."
- Marcus Aurelius, Meditations 5:20

Marcus Aurelius teaches us to view professional challenges as opportunities for growth.

The mind can reframe obstacles as pathways to develop resilience, creativity, and problem-solving skills.

Stoic Affirmation for today:

"I embrace professional challenges as opportunities to strengthen and refine my abilities."

Stoic Meditation:

Consider a current challenge at work. How can this perspective transform it into a growth opportunity?

DAY 68: LEADERSHIP AND STOICISM

"Never esteem anything as of advantage to you that will make you break your word or lose your self-respect."
- Marcus Aurelius, Meditations 3:7

Marcus Aurelius highlights the Stoic principles vital for leadership: integrity and self-respect. A true leader values these virtues above personal gain or acclaim.

Stoic Affirmation for today:

"In my role as a leader, I uphold integrity and self-respect, setting an example for others."

Stoic Meditation:

As a leader, how can maintaining your integrity and self-respect guide your decisions and actions today?

DAY 69:
AMBITION AND CONTENTMENT

Marcus Aurelius advises finding a balance between ambition and contentment. True contentment comes from within, based on our actions and choices, not external validation or achievements.

Stoic Affirmation for today:

"I pursue my ambitions with diligence, but anchor my contentment in my actions and personal values."

Stoic Meditation:

Reflect on how balancing ambition with inner contentment can lead to a more fulfilling and peaceful life.

DAY 70:
WEEKLY REFLECTION ON WORK

As we reflect on this week's focus on work, Marcus Aurelius reminds us to align our professional efforts with our core values and natural virtues.

Stoic Affirmation for today:

"I review my week's work, assessing how well it aligns with my fundamental virtues and values."

Stoic Meditation:

Consider the past week's work. How did your efforts and attitude reflect your personal principles and contribute to your growth?

DAY 71: UNDERSTANDING OUR EMOTIONS

Marcus Aurelius teaches that emotions stem from our perceptions. Understanding this empowers us to manage our emotions more effectively.

Stoic Affirmation for today:

"I examine my emotions to understand their roots in my perceptions, gaining mastery over my reactions."

Stoic Meditation:

Reflect on a recent strong emotion. How did your perception influence this feeling?

DAY 72:
THE STOIC AND ANGER

"How much more harmful are the consequences of anger... than the circumstances that aroused it in us."
- Marcus Aurelius, Meditations 11:18

Marcus Aurelius warns about the destructiveness of anger. Recognizing this can help us respond with reason rather than emotion.

Stoic Affirmation for today:

"I choose to respond to provocation with calmness and reason, not anger."

Stoic Meditation:

Think of a recent moment of anger. How might a calm response have altered the outcome?

DAY 73:

STOICISM AND FEAR

Marcus Aurelius challenges us to confront our fears, emphasizing that the true loss is in not fully living. Stoicism teaches us to face fear with courage and rationality.

Stoic Affirmation for today:

"I face my fears with courage, choosing to live fully and purposefully."

Stoic Meditation:

Identify a fear holding you back. How can confronting it enhance your life?

DAY 74: DEALING WITH SADNESS

"Be not swept off your feet by the vividness of the impression, but say, 'Impression, wait for me a little. Let me see what you are and what you represent. Let me try you.'"
- Marcus Aurelius, Meditations 11:37

Aurelius teaches us to examine our emotions, including sadness, before reacting. This reflection allows us to understand and address the root causes more effectively.

Stoic Affirmation for today:

"I observe my sadness with patience and clarity, seeking to understand its source and respond thoughtfully."

Stoic Meditation:

When you feel sadness, pause to explore its origin and what it can teach you.

DAY 75:
ENVY AND JEALOUSY

"The soul becomes dyed with the color of its thoughts."
- Marcus Aurelius, Meditations 5:16

Marcus Aurelius reminds us that envy and jealousy harm not only our well-being but also the collective harmony. Cultivating contentment on our own path is key.

Stoic Affirmation for today:
"I focus on my journey, finding contentment within and rejecting feelings of envy and jealousy."

Stoic Meditation:
Consider an instance of envy or jealousy. How can shifting focus to your own growth and accomplishments alleviate these feelings?

DAY 76:
EUPHORIA AND EQUANIMITY

"Pleasures, when they go beyond a certain limit, are but punishments."
- Marcus Aurelius, Meditations 6:24

Marcus Aurelius cautions against the excesses of euphoria, suggesting a balanced approach to life's highs.

True equanimity is found in moderation, not in extreme emotional states.

Stoic Affirmation for today:
"I seek balance in my emotions, finding peace in equanimity rather than in extreme euphoria."

Stoic Meditation:
Reflect on a moment of intense joy that came before an intense low. How can maintaining a balanced perspective enhance your overall well-being?

DAY 77:
WEEKLY REFLECTION ON EMOTIONS

"If you are pained by any external thing, it is not this thing that disturbs you, but your own judgment about it. And it is in your power to wipe out this judgment now."
- Marcus Aurelius, Meditations 8:47

In this week's focus on emotions, Marcus Aurelius guides us to understand how our judgments influence our feelings. Recognizing this power can lead to greater emotional mastery.

Stoic Affirmation for today:

"I reflect on how my judgments have shaped my emotions this week, and I embrace the power to change these perceptions for inner peace."

Stoic Meditation:

Think about instances this week when your judgment affected your emotions. How can altering these judgments improve your emotional well-being?

DAY 78:
THE EXAMINATION OF CONSCIENCE

"At day's end, when you're most tired, question yourself: What good did I do today?
How can I improve?"
- Marcus Aurelius, Meditations 10:11

Marcus Aurelius encourages a daily examination of conscience, a reflection on our actions and their alignment with our moral values. This introspection is crucial for personal growth and ethical living.

Stoic Affirmation for today:
"I end each day with self-reflection, evaluating my actions and seeking ways to grow and improve."

Stoic Meditation:
Tonight, review your day: What good did you do? Where can you improve?

DAY 79:
THE DAILY REVIEW

Marcus Aurelius emphasizes the importance of constant self-awareness and evaluation.

The daily review is a practice of questioning our actions and choices to ensure they align with our essential values and goals.

Stoic Affirmation for today:
"I regularly assess my actions and decisions, ensuring they align with my core values and life's objectives."

Stoic Meditation:
Throughout today, pause to reflect on your actions. Are they necessary and aligned with your values?

DAY 80:
JOURNALING AS A TOOL

"At dawn, when you have trouble getting out of bed, tell yourself: 'I have to go to work — as a human being. What do I have to complain of, if I'm going to do what I was born for — the things I was brought into the world to do? Or is this what I was created for? To huddle under the blankets and stay warm?'"
\- Marcus Aurelius, Meditations 5:1

This message reflects on the importance of self-discipline and purpose, themes relevant to the practice of journaling.
By documenting our thoughts and responsibilities, we reinforce our commitment to our duties and self-improvement.

Stoic Affirmation for today:
"I use journaling to clarify my purpose and responsibilities, committing to my role as a human being striving for virtue."

Stoic Meditation:
Reflect on how journaling can help you stay focused on your responsibilities and personal growth.

DAY 81:
THE ROLE OF WRITING IN STOICISM

Marcus Aurelius illustrates how he used writing as a tool for motivation and self-examination. Writing not only captures thoughts but also serves as a medium for clarifying purpose and reinforcing commitment to one's duties.

Stoic Affirmation for today:
"Through writing, I find clarity and purpose, reinforcing my commitment to my duties and personal growth."

Stoic Meditation:
Consider how writing can help you clarify and reaffirm your daily purpose and goals.

DAY 82:
STOIC MEDITATION AND REFLECTION

"Withdraw into yourself and look. And if you do not find yourself beautiful yet, act as does the creator of a statue that is to be made beautiful: he cuts away here, he smooths there, he makes this line lighter, this other purer, until a lovely face has grown upon his work."

- Marcus Aurelius, Meditations 5:3

Marcus Aurelius highlights the importance of self-reflection and personal development, akin to an artist perfecting a sculpture.

This practice of reviewing and contemplating our thoughts and actions is crucial for personal growth and aligning ourselves with Stoic virtues.

Stoic Affirmation for today:

"I continuously refine my character through self-reflection, aspiring to beauty in virtue and thought."

Stoic Meditation:

Consider areas of your life that could benefit from this sculptor's approach. How can introspection and mindful adjustments improve your character and actions?

DAY 83: CLARIFYING THOUGHTS THROUGH WRITING

"Be content to seem what you really are."
- Marcus Aurelius, Meditations 10:16

Marcus Aurelius emphasizes the virtue of authenticity, a quality that can be cultivated through reflective writing. Writing helps in clarifying thoughts, understanding oneself, and embracing genuineness.

Stoic Affirmation for today:
"Through writing, I explore and express my true self, fostering authenticity in my thoughts and actions."

Stoic Meditation:
Engage in a writing exercise focused on a recent experience. How did it reflect your true self? How can writing help you understand and align your actions with your authentic values?

DAY 84:
WEEKLY REFLECTION ON PRACTICE

"How have I erred, what done or left undone? So start each day."
- Marcus Aurelius, Meditations 8:2

End your week with a Stoic reflection on actions and omissions, aligning with Aurelius's practice of daily self-assessment.

Stoic Affirmation for today:

"I reflect on my weekly deeds, acknowledging virtues practiced and recognizing areas for improvement."

Stoic Meditation:

Reflect on your actions this past week. Where did you live up to Stoic ideals, what mistakes did you make, where did you fail, and what can be improved?

DAY 85:
THE NATURAL ORDER

"Observe constantly that all things take place through change, and accustom thyself to consider that the nature of the Universe loves nothing so much as to change the things which are and to make new things like them."
- Marcus Aurelius, Meditations 4:35

Here, Marcus Aurelius teaches the acceptance of change as a natural order of the universe.

Stoic Affirmation for today:

"I embrace change as a natural and essential part of life and the universe."

Stoic Meditation:

Reflect on a recent change in your life. How does viewing it as a natural process alter your perspective?

DAY 86:
LIVING ACCORDING TO NATURE

"Frequently consider the connection of all things in the universe and their relation to one another."
- Marcus Aurelius, Meditations 6:38

Marcus Aurelius urges us to contemplate our place in the natural order, encouraging a life in harmony with the world around us.

Stoic Affirmation for today:
"I seek to live in harmony with nature, understanding my connection to the universe and its rhythms."

Stoic Meditation:
Today, ponder your actions. How do they align with the natural world and its interconnected systems?

DAY 87:
THE RHYTHM OF LIFE

"Everything is interwoven, and the web is holy."
- Marcus Aurelius, Meditations 7:9

Marcus Aurelius reflects on the interconnectedness of life, emphasizing that each part of the universe, including ourselves, moves in a harmonious rhythm.

Stoic Affirmation for today:

"I recognize and respect the interwoven rhythms of life, finding my place within its harmony."

Stoic Meditation:

Consider how your daily actions and decisions are part of life's greater rhythm. How can you more consciously align with this flow?

DAY 88:
NATURE'S LESSONS

Reflect on nature's resilience and constant evolution for guidance and inspiration.

Stoic Affirmation for today:

"I draw lessons from nature, embracing its resilience and adaptability in my life."

Stoic Meditation:

Observe a natural element today. What can it teach you about persistence or adaptation?

DAY 89:
THE UNIVERSE WITHIN

"Look within. Within is the fountain of good, and it will ever bubble up, if thou wilt ever dig."
- Marcus Aurelius, Meditations 7:59

Marcus Aurelius encourages us to explore our inner selves, reminding us that the source of goodness and understanding lies within.

Stoic Affirmation for today:

"I delve into my inner self, discovering the wellspring of goodness and wisdom that guides my understanding of the world."

Stoic Meditation:

Reflect on your inner exploration. How does understanding yourself better help you comprehend the world? How well do you really know your true Self?

DAY 90:
ECOLOGY AND STOICISM

Marcus Aurelius here illustrates the Stoic principle of interconnectedness, akin to ecology, where the well-being of each part contributes to the health of the whole system.

Stoic Affirmation for today:

"I recognize my role in the larger ecosystem, understanding that my actions impact the collective well-being."

Stoic Meditation:

Reflect on how your actions affect the environment and society. What changes can you make for a more harmonious impact?

DAY 91: WEEKLY REFLECTION ON NATURE

"Constantly regard the universe as one living being, having one substance and one soul."
- Marcus Aurelius, Meditations 4:40

As we reflect on this week's theme of aligning with nature, Marcus Aurelius's words remind us of our deep connection with the universe.

This week has been about understanding the rhythm of life, our role within the natural world, and how our inner universe mirrors the larger one.

Stoic Affirmation for today:
"I reflect on my interconnectedness with nature and the universe, recognizing how this understanding influences my actions and perspectives."

Stoic Meditation:
Consider this week's lessons from nature. How have they deepened your understanding of your place in the world?

DAY 92:
PREMEDITATION OF EVILS

"Begin each day by telling yourself: Today I shall be meeting with interference, ingratitude, insolence, disloyalty, ill-will, and selfishness."
- Marcus Aurelius, Meditations 2:1

Marcus Aurelius advocates the practice of *premeditatio malorum*, or the premeditation of evils, as a way to mentally prepare for life's challenges.

By anticipating difficulties, we can strengthen our resilience and maintain composure when faced with adversity.

Stoic Affirmation for today:
"I mentally prepare for life's challenges, fortifying my resilience and composure."

Stoic Meditation:
Reflect on potential challenges you might face today. How can this forethought help you respond with calmness and clarity?

DAY 93:
THE STOIC'S ARMOR

"You have power over your mind — not outside events. Realize this, and you will find strength."
- Marcus Aurelius, Meditations 6:41

Marcus Aurelius emphasizes the importance of mental fortitude.

The Stoic's armor lies in controlling one's thoughts and reactions, making them impervious to external turmoil.

This mindset is a source of inner strength.

Stoic Affirmation for today:
"I fortify my mind, understanding that my power lies in how I perceive and respond to the world around me."

Stoic Meditation:
Today, focus on cultivating mental resilience. How does controlling your reactions strengthen your emotional and psychological armor?

DAY 94: FACING FEARS

Marcus Aurelius challenges us to confront our fears, emphasizing that the greatest fear should be a life unlived.

By facing our fears, we open ourselves to growth and the richness of experience.

Stoic Affirmation for today:

"I confront my fears with courage, understanding that true living is found beyond the boundaries of comfort."

Stoic Meditation:

Identify a fear you face. How can embracing this challenge lead to a fuller, more engaged life?

DAY 95:
CRISIS AND CHARACTER

In times of crisis, Marcus Aurelius advises us to maintain our integrity and character.

How we respond to adversity is a true test of our virtues and values.

Stoic Affirmation for today:

"In the face of crisis, I uphold my character and virtues, responding with integrity and resilience."

Stoic Meditation:

Reflect on a recent challenge. How did your response align with your core values and character?

DAY 96:
THE UNKNOWN AND THE UNCONTROLLABLE

Marcus Aurelius reminds us that our distress about the unknown or uncontrollable stems from our perceptions.

By changing our perspective, we can reduce our anxiety and maintain calm.

Stoic Affirmation for today:

"I choose to view the unknown and uncontrollable with equanimity, focusing on my reactions, which are within my control."

Stoic Meditation:

Reflect on a situation beyond your control. How can altering your perception of it change your emotional response?

DAY 97: ANTICIPATING CHALLENGES

"Do not be terrified by the thought of being overpowered by another. For not only does the semblance of honor not constitute a good, but neither does life, nor yet the loss of life constitute an evil."

\- Marcus Aurelius, Meditations 11:18

Marcus Aurelius advises facing potential challenges with a calm and balanced perspective. Recognizing that life's ups and downs do not define our core worth allows us to meet challenges with equanimity.

Stoic Affirmation for today:

"I face anticipated challenges with calmness and clarity, knowing that external events do not define my inner worth."

Stoic Meditation:

Consider a challenge you may soon face. How can maintaining a balanced perspective help you navigate it effectively?

DAY 98:
WEEKLY REFLECTION ON ADVERSITY

Reflecting on the week, Marcus Aurelius reminds us to appreciate life even amidst adversity. This week's focus on challenges and how we respond to them underscores the importance of resilience and perspective.

Stoic Affirmation for today:

"I reflect on the adversities of this week, appreciating the lessons and strength gained from each challenge."

Stoic Meditation:

Consider the adversities you faced this week. How have they contributed to your growth and understanding of life's preciousness?

DAY 99: THE VALUE OF ASCETIC EXERCISES

"Set yourself free from the judgment of others."
- Marcus Aurelius

Marcus Aurelius suggests that ascetic practices, like freeing oneself from the concern of others' judgments, are valuable for cultivating Stoicism.

These exercises strengthen our resilience and independence.

Stoic Affirmation for today:

"I engage in practices that strengthen my self-reliance and inner fortitude, freeing myself from the undue influence of external judgments."

Stoic Meditation:

Consider an ascetic practice you can adopt today. How might it bolster your Stoic journey?

DAY 100:
MINIMALISM AND PURPOSE

Marcus Aurelius highlights the essence of minimalism — finding contentment and happiness not in external possessions, but within oneself and one's thoughts. This perspective emphasizes the importance of purpose over material abundance.

Stoic Affirmation for today:

"I embrace minimalism, finding joy and purpose in simplicity and the richness of my inner world."

Stoic Meditation:

Reflect on how adopting a minimalist approach can enhance your focus on purpose and personal fulfillment.

DAY 101:
SELF-DENIAL AND STRENGTH

"You have power over your mind – not outside events. Realize this, and you will find strength."
- Marcus Aurelius, Meditations 6:41

Marcus Aurelius teaches the power of self-denial as a form of mental discipline. By focusing on controlling our mind and reactions, rather than external circumstances, we cultivate inner strength.

Stoic Affirmation for today:

"I exercise self-denial as a means to strengthen my mind, focusing on what I can control – my thoughts and responses."

Stoic Meditation:

Today, practice self-denial in a small way. How does this act of discipline strengthen your mental fortitude?

DAY 102:
LUXURY AND EXCESS

Marcus Aurelius reminds us that indulgence in luxury and excess can clutter our minds, detracting from the quality of our thoughts and inner life. A focus on simplicity helps maintain mental clarity and purpose.

Stoic Affirmation for today:

"I choose simplicity over excess, understanding that a clear mind and purposeful living are my true luxuries."

Stoic Meditation:

Reflect on the impact of luxury and excess in your life. How does simplifying your desires and lifestyle benefit your mental well-being and clarity?

DAY 103:
DISCIPLINE OF DESIRE

"If you set yourself to your present task along the path of true reason, with all determination, vigor, and good will; if you admit no distraction, but keep your own divinity in clear view; if you stay true to this, expecting nothing, fearing nothing, but satisfied with your present activity according to nature... you will live happily. And there is no man who is able to prevent this."
- Marcus Aurelius, Meditations 3:12

Marcus Aurelius highlights the discipline of desire. By focusing on the present task and aligning with reason, we can find true contentment.

Stoic Affirmation for today:
"I practice applying discipline to my desires, focusing on the present and aligning my actions with reason."

Stoic Meditation:
Consider how disciplining your desires can lead to a more focused and fulfilling life. What can you do today to practice this?

DAY 104: ENJOYMENT IN MODERATION

Marcus Aurelius advises enjoying life's pleasures with moderation and discernment. True excellence of character lies in balanced living, embracing joys wisely and in measure.

Stoic Affirmation for today:

"I find enjoyment in moderation, understanding that the excellence of my character is reflected in my balanced approach to life's pleasures."

Stoic Meditation:

Reflect on how you can enjoy life's pleasures today in a way that is balanced and moderate. How does this enhance the quality of your experience and character?

DAY 105:
WEEKLY REFLECTION ON ASCETICISM

As we reflect on this week's focus on asceticism, Marcus Aurelius's words remind us of the value of simplicity and contentment.

Embracing what we have and curbing excessive desires can lead to a profound sense of fulfillment and peace.

Stoic Affirmation for today:

"I reflect on the lessons of simplicity and restraint this week, appreciating their role in cultivating a contented and peaceful life."

Stoic Meditation:

Consider how practicing asceticism this week has impacted your sense of contentment and well-being. What have you learned about your needs versus your wants?

DAY 106:
BEING CONTENT WITH LITTLE

Marcus Aurelius conveys the idea that true contentment doesn't come from abundance but from a state of mind that finds satisfaction in simplicity.

Stoic Affirmation for today:

"I find richness in simplicity and am content with the essentials, understanding they provide true fulfillment."

Stoic Meditation:

Reflect on aspects of your life where less is more. How does embracing minimalism bring you peace and contentment?

DAY 107:
WEALTH AND HAPPINESS

"Wealth consists not in having great possessions, but in having few wants."
- Marcus Aurelius, Meditations 7:33

Marcus Aurelius highlights that true wealth lies in contentment and simplicity rather than in the abundance of possessions.

Happiness is found in wanting less, rather than in accumulating more.

Stoic Affirmation for today:

"I measure wealth not by my possessions, but by my ability to live contently with less."

Stoic Meditation:

Reflect on the difference between your needs and wants. How does this perspective influence your understanding of wealth and happiness?

DAY 108:
AUTARKY

"Your happiness depends on three things, all of which are within your power: your will, your ideas concerning the events in which you are involved, and the use you make of your ideas."
- Marcus Aurelius, Meditations 11:18

Marcus Aurelius teaches the value of autarky, or self-sufficiency, emphasizing that true happiness is achieved through internal control over one's will and perceptions, rather than external circumstances.

Stoic Affirmation for today:

"I seek happiness through self-sufficiency, controlling my will and perceptions, independent of external events."

Stoic Meditation:

Today, focus on how your thoughts and attitudes, rather than external factors, can shape your happiness and contentment.

DAY 109:
THE TRUE VALUE OF THINGS

---

*"Everything we hear is an opinion, not a fact. Everything we see is
a perspective, not the truth."*
- Marcus Aurelius, Meditations 12:18

This reflection by Marcus Aurelius reminds us that the value we assign to things is subjective and often influenced by our perceptions and beliefs. Recognizing this can help us understand the true value of things in life.

Stoic Affirmation for today:
"I acknowledge that the value of things lies in my perception. I strive to see beyond superficial judgments to understand their true worth."

Stoic Meditation:
Reflect on something you recently valued highly. How does understanding its value from an objective perspective change your view of its importance?

DAY 110: INDEPENDENCE FROM MATERIALISM

"He who fears death will never do anything worthy of a man who is alive. But if you will be alive after death, you must die while you are alive."

- Marcus Aurelius, Meditations 4:19

Marcus Aurelius encourages living a life of substance, implying that an overemphasis on materialism can detract from truly meaningful experiences. True independence comes from focusing on deeper values and purposes, rather than material possessions.

Stoic Affirmation for today:

"I seek a life rich in experience and virtue, not in material possessions. My independence lies in my values and actions."

Stoic Meditation:

Contemplate how reducing your focus on material possessions can free you to pursue more meaningful aspects of life.

DAY 111:
CONTENTMENT IN ACTION

"Just that you do the right thing. The rest doesn't matter."
- Marcus Aurelius, Meditations 6:2

Marcus Aurelius emphasizes that contentment comes from doing what is right and virtuous, rather than from external achievements or recognition.

True satisfaction is found in the action itself and in aligning with one's ethical principles.

Stoic Affirmation for today:

"I find contentment in acting rightly and virtuously, independent of external outcomes or rewards."

Stoic Meditation:

Reflect on how taking the right action, regardless of its recognition or reward, brings a deeper sense of fulfillment and contentment.

DAY 112:
WEEKLY REFLECTION ON CONTENTMENT

"Very little is needed to make a happy life; it is all within yourself, in your way of thinking."
- Marcus Aurelius, Meditations 7:67

Reflecting on the week, Marcus Aurelius's words remind us that contentment comes from within, shaped by our attitudes and perceptions, not by external circumstances or possessions.

Stoic Affirmation for today:

"I reflect on this week's moments of contentment, recognizing they stem from my thoughts and attitudes, not from external factors."

Stoic Meditation:

Consider the past week: How did your mindset influence your sense of contentment? What can you learn from these reflections for the coming week?

DAY 113:
THE JUST LIFE

"Justice consists in doing no injury to men; decency in giving them no offense."
- Marcus Aurelius, Meditations 9:1

Marcus Aurelius defines justice not just as the absence of harm, but also as the presence of respect and decency towards others.

Living a just life involves actively considering the impact of our actions on those around us.

Stoic Affirmation for today:
"I commit to living justly, ensuring my actions cause no harm and respect the dignity of others."

Stoic Meditation:
Reflect on your actions today. How can you ensure they align with the principles of justice and decency?

DAY 114:
LAWS AND MORALS

"Just as law is set over the magistrate, even so are the magistrates set over the people. And therefore, in a certain way, the law is over the gods, for it is they who obey the law."
- Marcus Aurelius, Meditations 12:5

Marcus Aurelius draws a connection between laws, moral authority, and governance.

He suggests that even those in power are subject to the laws of morality and justice.

Stoic Affirmation for today:

"I respect and uphold laws, recognizing their role in maintaining moral order and justice."

Stoic Meditation:

Consider how adherence to both legal and moral laws guides your actions and contributes to a just society.

DAY 115:
THE SOCIAL CONTRACT

"What injures the hive, injures the bee."
- Marcus Aurelius, Meditations 6:54

Marcus Aurelius alludes to the concept of a social contract, emphasizing our interconnectedness and the impact of individual actions on the community.

By acknowledging our role within this larger social structure, we recognize the importance of contributing positively to the collective.

Stoic Affirmation for today:

"I acknowledge my part in the social contract, striving to act in ways that benefit the broader community."

Stoic Meditation:

Reflect on your actions and their impact on society. How can you ensure they contribute positively to the collective well-being?

DAY 116:
ACTIONS AND THEIR RIPPLE EFFECTS

"Whatever happens to you has been waiting to happen since the beginning of time. The twining strands of fate wove both of them together: your own existence and the things that happen to you."
- Marcus Aurelius, Meditations 5:8

Marcus Aurelius suggests that our actions are intertwined with the fabric of fate, reminding us that everything we do creates ripples that affect the broader tapestry of life.

Stoic Affirmation for today:
"I am mindful of the ripple effects of my actions, understanding their impact on the greater whole."

Stoic Meditation:
Consider a recent action and its wider consequences. How does this awareness influence your future choices?

DAY 117:
FAIRNESS IN PRACTICE

"Just as it is a good thing to be just, so it is a bad thing to be unjust. I am not saying this with reference to the external world, but with regard to what is inside us: it is bad for you to have an unjust soul."
- Marcus Aurelius, Meditations 9:1

Marcus Aurelius emphasizes the internal value of fairness. True justice is intrinsic, reflecting the state of one's soul.

It's essential to practice fairness, not just as an external duty but as a core aspect of one's character, impacting all interactions, especially those where power dynamics, like employer-employee relationships, come into play.

Stoic Affirmation for today:

"I uphold fairness in all my dealings, recognizing it as a reflection of my inner character and integrity, especially in positions of responsibility and authority."

Stoic Meditation:

Reflect on areas in your life, particularly in professional or leadership roles, where you can more deeply embody fairness.

Consider the long-term impact of fairness on your character and those you interact with.

DAY 118:
STOICISM IN LEADERSHIP

"The best kind of revenge is to be unlike him who performed the injustice."

\- Marcus Aurelius, Meditations 6:6

Marcus Aurelius encourages leaders to embody Stoicism by acting with integrity and virtue, especially in the face of injustice or wrongdoing.

True leadership involves setting a higher standard and being an example of ethical behavior.

Stoic Affirmation for today:

"As a leader, I commit to acting with integrity and virtue, setting a positive example for those I lead."

Stoic Meditation:

Reflect on your role as a leader. How can you demonstrate Stoic virtues in your leadership to positively influence and guide others?

DAY 119:
WEEKLY REFLECTION ON JUSTICE AND SOCIETY

As we conclude our week focusing on justice and society, Marcus Aurelius reminds us of our interconnectedness and the impact of our actions on the greater whole. This week has been about understanding the role of fairness, equity, and leadership in contributing to a just society.

Stoic Affirmation for today:

"I reflect on my actions this week, considering how they have contributed to justice and the well-being of society."

Stoic Meditation:

Consider your impact on society this week. How have your actions and decisions promoted justice and fairness? What can you learn from these reflections for the future?

DAY 120:
LOOKING FORWARD AND BACKWARD

"Remember how long you have been putting off these things, and how often you have received an opportunity from the gods, and yet do not use it."
- Marcus Aurelius, Meditations 2:4

On this final day, reflect comprehensively on your journey through these Stoic teachings. Look back at the lessons learned, the virtues practiced, and the insights gained.

Stoic Affirmation for today:

"I review my Stoic journey with gratitude, ready to apply these principles to future challenges and opportunities."

Stoic Meditation:

Reflect on your growth throughout this journey. How will you apply the Stoic principles you've learned to future situations?

Consider setting specific goals or intentions that align with your newfound insights and understanding.

Conclusion

As you conclude this 120-day journey through the teachings of Marcus Aurelius and Stoic philosophy, you will carry forward with you timeless wisdom that is as relevant today as it was in ancient times.

The core Stoic virtues – wisdom, courage, justice, and temperance – have been your guides, offering a framework for living a life of purpose, integrity, and resilience.

Wisdom has shown you the importance of discernment, learning from experiences, and seeing the world through a lens of reason and understanding.

Courage has encouraged you to face life's challenges with strength and conviction, teaching you that true bravery is found in the mastery of one's fears and the willingness to grow.

Justice has reminded you of your connection to others, emphasizing fairness, empathy, and the impact of your actions on the broader community.

And **Temperance**, or moderation, has taught you the value of self-control and the power of balancing life's pleasures with responsibility and restraint.

Throughout this journey, you've learned that happiness and contentment come from within – they are states of being that you cultivate through your thoughts, actions, and reactions to the world around you.

You've discovered the strength in accepting what you cannot change and the power in focusing on what lies within your control.

As you move forward, carry these lessons with you. Let them be your compass as you navigate the complexities of life.

Remember that every challenge is an opportunity for growth, every interaction a chance to practice virtue, and every moment an invitation to live fully and mindfully.

Your Stoic journey does not end here. It is an ongoing practice, a continual return to these principles as you grow and evolve.

With each day, you have the chance to live more fully in accordance with these timeless virtues, building a life of meaning, fulfillment, and tranquility.

Final Words of Encouragement:

You are now equipped with the tools and insights to face life's journey with a Stoic heart and mind.

Embrace the path ahead with curiosity, openness, and the assurance that, whatever life brings, you have within you the wisdom, strength, and character to meet it with grace and virtue.

Your journey continues, and each step is an opportunity to manifest the best version of yourself, for your benefit and for the good of all.

Remember, in the words of Marcus Aurelius, *"The best revenge is to be unlike him who performed the injustice."*

Go forth with the tranquility and resolve of a true Stoic.

About the Author

Charles Abbott is an American writer with a passion for philosophy and social sciences based on human thought processes and behaviors.

Abbott's writing is focused on personal development, mindset, and health in the modern world. He lives with his wife and two children in Austin, Texas.

Please Leave a 5-Star Review

If you enjoyed this book, please leave a positive review to help more readers discover Stoicism. Your review will help others because by applying the powerful Stoic principles, they too can lead happier lives.